mouthmark series

Teaching My Mother How To Give Birth

literary pointillism on a funked-out canvas

Teaching My Mother How To Give Birth

mouthmark series (No. 10)
Printed and Bound in the United Kingdom

Published by the mouthmark series, 2011
the pamphlet series of flipped eye publishing
All Rights Reserved

First Edition
Copyright © Warsan Shire 2011

Cover Design by Effi Ibok
Series Design © flipped eye publishing, 2009

ISBN-10: 1-905233-29-9
ISBN-13: 978-1-905233-29-8

LOTTERY FUNDED

Mother, loosen my tongue or adorn me with a lighter burden.
— Audre Lorde

Teaching My Mother How To Give Birth

Warsan Shire

mouthmark *poetry is a kind of literary pointillism applied on a jazz-blues-blood-sex-rock-and-rolled canvas with sweat, tears and spittle as primary colours; if you don't get it you're not listening...*

Contents

I have my mother's mouth and my father's eyes; on my face they are still together.

What Your Mother Told You
After Your Father Left

I did not beg him to stay
because I was begging God
that he would not leave.

Your Mother's First Kiss

The first boy to kiss your mother later raped women
when the war broke out. She remembers hearing this
from your uncle, then going to your bedroom and lying
down on the floor. You were at school.

Your mother was sixteen when he first kissed her.
She held her breath for so long that she blacked out.
On waking she found her dress was wet and sticking
to her stomach, half moons bitten into her thighs.

That same evening she visited a friend, a girl
who fermented wine illegally in her bedroom.
When your mother confessed *I've never been touched
like that before*, the friend laughed, mouth bloody with grapes,
then plunged a hand between your mother's legs.

Last week, she saw him driving the number 18 bus,
his cheek a swollen drumlin, a vine scar dragging itself
across his mouth. You were with her, holding a bag
of dates to your chest, heard her let out a deep moan
when she saw how much you looked like him.

Things We Had Lost in the Summer

The summer my cousins return from Nairobi,
we sit in a circle by the oak tree in my aunt's garden.
They look older. Amel's hardened nipples push through
the paisley of her blouse, minarets calling men to worship.
When they left, I was twelve years old and swollen
with the heat of waiting. We hugged at the departure gate,
waifs with bird chests clinking like wood, boyish,
long skirted figurines waiting to grow
into our hunger.

My mother uses her quiet voice on the phone:
Are they all okay? Are they healing well?
She doesn't want my father to overhear.

Juwariyah, my age, leans in and whispers
I've started my period. Her hair is in my mouth when
I try to move in closer– *how does it feel?*
She turns to her sisters and a laugh that is not hers
stretches from her body like a moan.
She is more beautiful than I can remember.
One of them pushes my open knees closed.
Sit like a girl. I finger the hole in my shorts,
shame warming my skin.

In the car, my mother stares at me through the
rear view mirror, the leather sticks to the back of my
thighs. I open my legs like a well-oiled door,
daring her to look at me and give me
what I had not lost: a name.

Maymuun's Mouth

Maymuun lost her accent with the help of her local Community College. Most evenings she calls me long distance to discuss the pros and cons of heating molasses in the microwave to remove body hair. Her new voice is sophisticated. She has taken to dancing in front of strangers. She lives next door to a Dominican who speaks to her in Spanish whenever they pass each other in hallways. I know she smiles at him, front teeth stained from the fluoride in the water back home. She's experiencing new things. We understand. We've received the photos of her standing by a bridge, the baby hair she'd hated all her life slicked down like ravines. Last week her answering machine picked up. I imagined her hoisted by the waist, wearing stockings, learning to kiss with her new tongue.

Grandfather's Hands

Your grandfather's hands were brown.
Your grandmother kissed each knuckle,

circled an island into his palm
and told him which parts they would share,
which part they would leave alone.

She wet a finger to draw where the ocean would be
on his wrist, kissed him there,
named the ocean after herself.

Your grandfather's hands were slow but urgent.
Your grandmother dreamt them,

a clockwork of fingers finding places to own—
under the tongue, collarbone, bottom lip,
arch of foot.

Your grandmother names his fingers after seasons—
index finger, a wave of heat,
middle finger, rainfall.

Some nights his thumb is the moon
nestled just under her rib.

Your grandparents often found themselves
in dark rooms, mapping out
each other's bodies,

claiming whole countries
with their mouths.

Bone

I find a girl the height of a small wail
living in our spare room. She looks the way I did when I was fifteen
full of pulp and pepper.
She spends all day up in the room
measuring her thighs.

Her body is one long sigh.
You notice her in the hallway.
Later that night while we lay beside one another
listening to her throw up in our bathroom,
you tell me you want to save her.
Of course you do;
This is what she does best:
makes you sick with the need
to help.

We have the same lips,
she and I,
the kind men think about
when they are with their wives.
She is starving.
You look straight at me when she tells us
how her father likes to punch girls
in the face.

I can hear you in our spare room with her.
What is she hungry for?
What can you fill her up with?
What can you do, that you would not do for me?
I count my ribs before I go to sleep.

Snow

My father was a drunk. He married my mother
the month he came back from Russia
with whiskey in his blood.
On their wedding night, he whispered
into her ear about jet planes and snow.
He said the word in Russian;
my mother blinked back tears and spread her palms
across his shoulder blades like the wings
of a plane. Later, breathless, he laid his head
on her thigh and touched her,
brought back two fingers glistening,
showed her from her own body
what the colour of snow was closest to.

Birds

Sofia used pigeon blood on her wedding night.
Next day, over the phone, she told me
how her husband smiled when he saw the sheets,

that he gathered them under his nose,
closed his eyes and dragged his tongue over the stain.
She mimicked his baritone, how he whispered

her name– Sofia,
pure, chaste, untouched.
We giggled over the static.

After he had praised her, she smiled, rubbed his head,
imagined his mother back home, parading
these siren sheets through the town,

waving at balconies, torso swollen with pride,
her arms fleshy wings bound to her body,
ignorant of flight.

Beauty

My older sister soaps between her legs, her hair
a prayer of curls. When she was my age, she stole
the neighbour's husband, burnt his name into her skin.
For weeks she smelt of cheap perfume and dying flesh.

It's 4 a.m. and she winks at me, bending over the sink,
her small breasts bruised from sucking.
She smiles, pops her gum before saying
boys are haram, don't ever forget that.

Some nights I hear her in her room screaming.
We play Surah Al-Baqarah to drown her out.
Anything that leaves her mouth sounds like sex.
Our mother has banned her from saying God's name.

The Kitchen

Half a papaya and a palmful of sesame oil;
    lately, your husband's mind has been elsewhere.

Honeyed dates, goat's milk;
    you want to quiet the bloating of salt.

Coconut and ghee butter;
    he kisses the back of your neck at the stove.

Cayenne and roasted pine nuts;
    you offer him the hollow of your throat.

Saffron and rosemary;
    you don't ask him her name.

Vine leaves and olives;
    you let him lift you by the waist.

Cinnamon and tamarind;
    lay you down on the kitchen counter.

Almonds soaked in rose water;
    your husband is hungry.

Sweet mangoes and sugared lemon;
    he had forgotten the way you taste.

Sour dough and cumin;
    but she cannot make him eat, like you.

Fire

The morning you were made to leave
she sat on the front steps,
dress tucked between her thighs,
a packet of Marlboro Lights
near her bare feet, painting her nails
until the polish curdled.
Her mother phoned–

What do you mean he hit you?
Your father hit me all the time
but I never left him.
He pays the bills
and he comes home at night,
what more do you want?

Later that night she picked the polish off
with her front teeth until the bed you shared
for seven years seemed speckled with glitter
and blood.

ii

On the drive to the hotel, you remember
the funeral you went to as a little boy,
double burial for a couple who
burned to death in their bedroom.
The wife had been visited
by her husband's lover,
a young and beautiful woman who paraded
her naked body in the couple's kitchen,
lifting her dress to expose breasts
mottled with small fleshy marks,
a back sucked and bruised, then dressed herself
and walked out of the front door.
The wife, waiting for her husband to come home,
doused herself in lighter fluid. On his arrival
she jumped on him, wrapping her legs around
his torso. The husband, surprised at her sudden urge,
carried his wife to the bedroom, where
she straddled him on their bed, held his face
against her chest and lit a match.

iii

A young man greets you in the elevator.
He smiles like he has pennies hidden in his cheeks.
You're looking at his shoes when he says
the rooms in this hotel are sweltering.
Last night in bed I swear I thought
my body was on fire.

When We Last Saw Your Father

He was sitting in the hospital parking lot
in a borrowed car, counting the windows
of the building, guessing which one
was glowing with his mistake.

You Were Conceived

On the night of our secret wedding
when he held me in his mouth like a promise
until his tongue grew tired and fell asleep,
I lay awake to keep the memory alive.

In the morning I begged him back to bed.
Running late, he kissed my ankles and left.
I stayed like a secret in his bed for days
until his mother found me.

I showed her my gold ring,
I stood in front of her naked,
waved my hands in her face.
She sank to the floor and cried.

At his funeral, no one knew my name.
I sat behind his aunts,
they sucked on dates soaked in oil.
The last thing he tasted was me.

Trying to Swim With God

Istaqfurulah

My mother says this city is slowly killing all our women;
practising back strokes at the local swimming pool.
I think of Kadija, how her body had failed her
on the way down from the block of flats.

The instructor tells us that the longest
a human being has held their breath under water
is 19 minutes and 21 seconds. At home in the bath,
my hair swells to the surface like vines, I stay submerged
until I can no longer stand it, think of all the things
I have allowed to slip through my fingers.

Inna lillahi Wa inna ilaihi Rajioon.

My mother says no one can fight it –
the body returning to God,

but the way she fell, face first,
in the dirt,
mouth full of earth,
 air, teeth, blood,
wearing a white cotton baati,
hair untied and smoked with ounsi,
I wonder if Kadija believed

she was going to float.

Questions for Miriam

Were you ever lonely?

Did you tell people that songs weren't
the same as a warm body, a soft mouth?
Did you know how to say no to young men
who cried outside your hotel rooms?
Did you listen to the songs they wrote,
tongues wet with praise for you?

What sweaty bars did you begin in?
Did you see them holding bottles by the neck,
hair on their arms rising as your notes hovered
above their heads?
Did you know of the girls who sang into their fists
mimicking your brilliance?

Did they know that you were only human?

My parents played your music at their wedding.
Called you Makeba, never Miriam, never first name,
always singer. Never wife, daughter, mother,
never lover, aching.

Did you tell people that songs weren't the same
as a warm body or a soft mouth? Miriam,
I've heard people using your songs as prayer,
begging god in falsetto. You were a city

exiled from skin, your mouth a burning church.

Conversations About Home
(at the Deportation Centre)

Well, I think home spat me out, the blackouts and curfews like tongue against loose tooth. God, do you know how difficult it is, to talk about the day your own city dragged you by the hair, past the old prison, past the school gates, past the burning torsos erected on poles like flags? When I meet others like me I recognise the longing, the missing, the memory of ash on their faces. No one leaves home unless home is the mouth of a shark. I've been carrying the old anthem in my mouth for so long that there's no space for another song, another tongue or another language. I know a shame that shrouds, totally engulfs. I tore up and ate my own passport in an airport hotel. I'm bloated with language I can't afford to forget.

*

They ask me *how did you get here?* Can't you see it on my body? The Libyan desert red with immigrant bodies, the Gulf of Aden bloated, the city of Rome with no jacket. I hope the journey meant more than miles because all of my children are in the water. I thought the sea was safer than the land. I want to make love, but my hair smells of war and running and running. I want to lay down, but these countries are like uncles who touch you when you're young and asleep. Look at all these borders, foaming at the mouth with bodies broken and desperate. I'm the colour of hot sun on the face, my mother's remains were never buried. I spent days and nights in the stomach of the truck; I did not come out the same. Sometimes it feels like someone else is wearing my body.

*

I know a few things to be true. I do not know where I am going, where I have come from is disappearing, I am unwelcome and my beauty is not beauty here. My body is burning with the shame of not belonging, my body is longing. I am the sin of memory and the absence of memory. I watch the news and my mouth becomes a sink full of blood. The lines, the forms, the people at the desks, the calling cards, the immigration officer, the looks on the street, the cold settling deep into my bones, the English classes at night, the distance I am from home. But Alhamdulilah all of this is better than the scent of a woman completely on fire, or a truckload of men who look like my father, pulling out my teeth and nails, or fourteen men between my legs, or a gun, or a promise, or a lie, or his name, or his manhood in my mouth.

*

I hear them say *go home*, I hear them say *fucking immigrants, fucking refugees*. Are they really this arrogant? Do they not know that stability is like a lover with a sweet mouth upon your body one second; the next you are a tremor lying on the floor covered in rubble and old currency waiting for its return. All I can say is, I was once like you, the apathy, the pity, the ungrateful placement and now my home is the mouth of a shark, now my home is the barrel of a gun. I'll see you on the other side.

Old Spice

Every Sunday afternoon he dresses in his old army uniform,
tells you the name of every man he killed.
His knuckles are unmarked graves.

Visit him on a Tuesday and he will describe
the body of every woman he could not save.
He'll say she looked like your mother
and you will feel a storm in your stomach.

Your grandfather is from another generation–
Russian degrees and a school yard Cuban national anthem,
communism and religion. Only music makes him cry now.

He married his first love, her with the long curls down
to the small of her back. Sometimes he would
pull her to him, those curls wrapped around his hand
like rope.

He lives alone now. Frail, a living memory
reclining in a seat, the room orbiting around him.
You visit him but never have anything to say.
When he was your age he was a man.
You retreat into yourself whenever he says your name.

Your mother's father,
the almost martyr,
can load a gun under water
in under four seconds.

Even his wedding night was a battlefield.
A Swiss knife, his young bride,

his sobs as he held Italian linen between her legs.

His face is a photograph left out in the sun,
the henna of his beard, the silver of his eyebrows
the wilted handkerchief, the kufi and the cane.

Your grandfather is dying.
He begs you *Take me home yaqay,*
I just want to see it one last time;
you don't know how to tell him that it won't be
anything like the way he left it.

My Foreign Wife is Dying and Does Not Want To Be Touched

My wife is a ship docking from war.
The doctor maps out her body in ink,
holding up her breast with two fingers, explains
what needs to be removed, that maybe we can keep
the nipple. Her body is a flooding home.
We are afraid. We want to know
what the water will take away from us,
what the earth will claim as its own.
I lick my lips and she looks at the floor.

Later, at home, she calls her sister.
They talk about curses, the evil eye, their aunt
who drowned, all the money they need
to send back. It is morning when she comes to bed
and lets me touch her. I am like a thirsty child
against her chest, her skin
is parchment, dry and cracking.

My wife sits on the hospital bed.
Gown and body together: 41 kilos.
She is a boat docking in from war,
her body, a burning village, a prison
with open gates. She won't let me hold her
now, when she needs it most.

We stare at the small television in the corner of the room.
I think of all the images she must carry in her body,
how the memory hardens into a tumour.
Apathy is the same as war,
it all kills you, she says.
Slow like cancer in the breast
or fast like a machete in the neck.

Ugly

Your daughter is ugly.
She knows loss intimately,
carries whole cities in her belly.

As a child, relatives wouldn't hold her.
She was splintered wood and sea water.
She reminded them of the war.

On her fifteenth birthday you taught her
how to tie her hair like rope
and smoke it over burning frankincense.

You made her gargle rosewater
and while she coughed, said
macaanto girls like you shouldn't smell
of lonely or empty.

You are her mother.
Why did you not warn her,
hold her like a rotting boat
and tell her that men will not love her
if she is covered in continents,
if her teeth are small colonies,
if her stomach is an island
if her thighs are borders?

What man wants to lie down
and watch the world burn
in his bedroom?

Your daughter's face is a small riot,

her hands are a civil war,
a refugee camp behind each ear,
a body littered with ugly things.

But God,
doesn't she wear
the world well?

Tea With Our Grandmothers

The morning your habooba died
I thought of my ayeeyo, the woman
I was named after, Warsan Baraka,
skin dark like tamarind flesh,
who died grinding cardamom
waiting for her sons to come home and
raise the loneliness they'd left behind;

or my mother's mother, Noura
with the honeyed laugh, who
broke cinnamon barks between
her palms, nursing her husband's
stroke, her sister's cancer and
her own bad back with broken
Swahili and stubborn Italian;

and Doris, the mother of your
English rose, named after
the daughter of Oceanus and Tethys
the Welsh in your blood, from the land
of Cymry, your grandmother who
dreams of clotted cream in her tea
through the swell of diabetes;

then your habooba Al-Sura,
God keep her, with three lines on
each cheek, a tally of surviving,
the woman who cooled your tea
pouring it like the weight of deeds
between bowl and cup, until the steam
would rise like a ghost.

In Love and In War

To my daughter I will say,
'when the men come, set yourself on fire'.

Notes

Surah Al Baqarah — A chapter in the Qu'ran, used to ward off evil.
Habooba — Arabic word meaning beloved woman, used as the word for grandmother in Sudan.
Ayeeyo — Somali word for Grandmother.
Macaanto — Somali term of endearment, meaning sweetness.
Inna lillahi Wa inna ilaihi Rajioon — Arabic; To Allah we belong and truly, to Him we shall return.
Baati — Long cotton Somali nightdress.
Ounsi — The somali tradition to burn frankincense and myrrh over hot coal, releasing aroma through smoke.
Istaqfurulah — Arabic, Allah forgive my sins.
Yaqay — Somali word used to emphasise emotion/urgency in speech.
Haram — Legally forbidden by Islamic law.
Kufi — A brimless short rounded cap worn mainly by African men.
Baraka — Blessings
Alhamdulilah — Praise be to Allah.

about Warsan Shire

Warsan Shire is a Kenyan-born Somali poet and writer who is based in London. Born in 1988, she is an artist and activist who uses her work to document narratives of journey and trauma. Warsan has read her work internationally, including recent readings in South Africa, Italy and Germany, and her poetry has been translated into Italian, Spanish and Portuguese.